Anchored in Love

Anchored in Love

Finding Peace in the Arms of My Father

A 28-Day Devotional Prayer Guide

Dr. Lynderia "Lyn" Cheevers Inah

Anchored in Love

Finding Peace in the Arms of My Father

A 28-Day Devotional Prayer Guide

Printed in the United States of America

Edited by Anita R. Minniefield

ISBN:979-8-9991860-0-3

Dedication

This devotional, Anchored in Love: *Finding Peace in the Arms of My Father,* is dedicated first and foremost to Abba, my Heavenly Father. Your love is the anchor that holds me steady through every season of life. Your faithfulness, grace, and mercy are the foundation on which I stand.

I also dedicate this book to the memory of my late father, Mr. Hilton Cheevers. You were dependable, steadfast, and faithful as a father. Your support and unwavering love mirrored the truth of 1 Peter 2:17 (NKJV): "Honor all people. Love the brotherhood. Fear God. Honor the king." You taught me by example, showed me what it meant to live with integrity, and demonstrated love in action every day. Though you are no longer with us, your legacy of love, strength, and HONOR continues to inspire me.

To my father in the Lord, Pastor Christopher Ibe, thank you for being a man of God who leads with integrity. Your teaching, compassion, and encouragement have been a beacon of light on my journey of faith. You have shown me what it means to walk closely with God, and your example has helped me grow in grace and truth.

May this devotional guide every reader to experience the unshakable love of our Heavenly Father, find peace in His arms, and remain anchored in His love through every circumstance of life.

With love and gratitude,

Lyn
Beloved Daughter of Kings

Foreword

Anchored In Love was not birthed out of a conference or seminary, it was birthed out of a secret place and a strong desire for intimacy with the Father. It was birthed out of Dr. Lyn's personal Garden of Gethsemane, where God crushed the Hannah anointing out of her to smear on those who use this devotional as a launching pad to the secret place with God. It was birthed from a place of personal life experiences that gives solid credibility to the prayers and to those who are in search of true intimacy with our Heavenly Father.

In a time when many are seeking answers through noise, platforms, and performance, this devotional invites the reader back to the stillness of the Father's arms—where healing flows and identity is affirmed. May those who read it receive the Hannah anointing with the ability and capacity to cry from the heart and release from your spiritual womb that which God had placed there before the foundations of the current earth's age.

The Hannah anointing speaks to a depth of intercession that births destiny and restores divine alignment. Dr. Lyn's obedience to steward such a sacred call through this 28-day journey is both courageous and catalytic.

Thank you, Dr. Lyn, for not passing the cup, but that the Father's Kingdom would come and that His will would be done in the earth as it is in Heaven.

To all who embark on this journey, may you encounter a love that anchors, heals, and revives.

Tony Brown,
L.E.E. Apostolic Network

A Note from the Author

"In all things showing yourself to be a pattern of good works; in doctrine showing integrity, reverence, incorruptibility." Titus 2:7 (NKJV)

This devotional was born out of deep love and personal conviction. When our son rededicated his life to the Lord on January 26, 2025, he expressed a longing to experience God's love in deeper dimensions. To support his journey, I committed to writing a devotional each day throughout February—Heart Month, a time when love is celebrated. What began as daily encouragement for our discussions became something more. I soon realized that many others could also benefit from this devotional as a resource to encounter the unfailing love of God in a greater way. This book is the result. You are holding in your hands something that was birthed out of love because of love.

To support accuracy and excellence, a neural network was used as a tool for copy editing, fact-checking, developmental editing, and proofreading. This allowed me to focus on the heart of the message while saving time and costs in production. As a mother and Minister of the Gospel with both a Doctorate and a Master of Divinity degree, I have written from experience, prayer, a deep commitment to edifying the Body of Christ, and a heartfelt desire for our son and future readers to truly know and experience the love of God in deeper dimensions. I have authored and published other works without the use of neural networks, and this publication is no different in spirit or intent.

Let there be no doubt: this work is the result of my personal labor, prayers, and study. It meets all legal and ethical standards for copyright and ownership. Above all, it reflects my sincere desire to see lives transformed by the immeasurable love of God. May this devotional guide you into a greater revelation of His love, for His love never fails (1 Corinthians 13:8).

In His Love,
Lyn C. Inah

Table of Contents

Introduction

Dearly Beloved Child of God, You are deeply loved. Before you took your first breath, God knew you and called you His own (Jeremiah 1:5). This 28-day devotional is a journey into the heart of God—a heart full of compassion, mercy, and never-ending love for you.

Life can be busy and full of distractions. Sometimes it's easy to forget just how much God loves you. But His love is not based on what you do or don't do. It is constant, pure, and unfailing. Romans 8:38-39 reminds us that nothing—absolutely nothing—can separate us from the love of God that is in Christ Jesus our Lord.

Each day in this devotional, you'll receive a gentle reminder of His love through Scripture, reflection, and a prayer. My prayer is that as you read, you will feel the arms of your Heavenly Father wrapping around you, comforting you, and strengthening your heart.

You are not alone on this journey. God is with you. His love will guide you, heal you, and restore your soul. Lean in, listen closely, and let His love wash over every part of your heart.

May these next 28 days draw you closer to the One who calls you "Beloved."

Seeing the Good in What God Has Made

"Then God saw everything that He had made, and indeed it was very good." —GENESIS 1:31

- God's love is shown through the beauty and goodness of His creation.

Devotional Illustration

Think about when you're working on a project that you're really passionate about—maybe it's fixing up a car, putting together a new playlist, or creating something in the studio. You put your heart and soul into it, and when you're done, you step back and look at what you've created. You feel proud. You know that what you made is something good. You see the effort, the care, and the skill you put into it, and it makes you appreciate what you've done even more.

In the same way, Genesis 1:31 tells us that when God finished creating the world, He looked at everything and said, "It was very good." This shows how much God loves His creation. He didn't just create the world and leave it there—He took time, He saw the beauty in everything He made, and He was proud of it. From the mountains to the oceans, the animals to people—everything was created with purpose and love.

Just like you feel pride in your work, God feels pride in His creation, including you. You are part of that "very good" world, made with care and purpose. Even when life gets tough, remember that you are created with love and that God sees the beauty in you. His love is reflected in everything around you, reminding you that He made you good, and He's proud of who you are.

Prayer

Lord, thank You for creating this beautiful world and for showing Your love through everything around us. Help us remember that we are part of Your "very good" creation. When life feels tough, remind us of the love and purpose You've placed in us. May we always see the beauty in ourselves and others. In Jesus' name. Amen.

Affirmations

1. I am wonderfully made by God, and He calls me "very good."
2. God's love is reflected in the beauty and goodness around me.
3. I was created with purpose and love by a perfect Creator.
4. In challenges, I remember I am an overcomer, built for this.
5. I choose to see the good in others, knowing they are also part of God's "very good" creation.

Anchor Thought: I am God's "very good" creation—seen, loved, and designed with purpose.

Reflection Questions

▶ How does the idea of God taking pride in His creation make you view yourself and others differently? Do you see yourself as part of God's "very good" creation?

_____

_____

_____

_____

_____

▶ In what ways can you recognize God's love through the beauty and goodness of the world around you? Can you think of a moment recently where you've seen this love reflected in nature or people?

_____

_____

_____

_____

_____

▶ When life gets challenging, how can remembering that you are made with purpose and love by God help you stay encouraged? How can this perspective change the way you handle difficulties?

_____

_____

_____

_____

_____

Day 2

Love That Never Gives Up

"And I will put enmity between you and the woman, and between your seed and her Seed; He shall bruise your head, and you shall bruise His heel." —Genesis 3:15

- Even in the fall, God promises a Savior, showing His love for humanity.

Devotional Illustration

Think about a time when you messed up—maybe you made a bad decision or found yourself in a place you knew you shouldn't be. You probably expected the worst: maybe rejection, judgment, or the end of a relationship. But instead, someone showed you love. They didn't pretend you hadn't messed up, but they didn't give up on you either. They still saw your worth.

That's exactly what God did for Adam and Eve after they sinned. They disobeyed God, and sin entered the world, bringing pain, brokenness, and separation from Him. But even in that moment of failure, God didn't turn His back on them. He made a promise—He would send a Savior. Someone who would crush the enemy's power and restore what was lost. That Savior is Jesus.

God's love is different from the love we see around us. Human love can be shaky, but God's love is unshakable. He knew we'd mess up, but He already had a plan to save us. That's real love—love that doesn't depend on how good we are but on who God is. No matter what you've done, His love for you hasn't changed. He's not waiting to give up on you; He's waiting to restore you.

Prayer

Lord, thank You for loving me even when I fall short. Thank You for sending Jesus to restore what was broken. Help me to trust in Your love, even when I don't feel worthy. Remind me that Your love never gives up on me. In Jesus' name, Amen.

Affirmations

1. God's love for me is unshakable, even when I mess up.
2. Jesus is proof that God's love never fails.
3. I am not defined by my mistakes—I am redeemed by God's grace.
4. God's plan for me is greater than my failures.
5. Nothing can separate me from the love of God.

Anchor Thought: God's love never gives up on me—even in my failure, He promised restoration.

Reflection Questions

▶ Have you ever experienced love and forgiveness when you didn't deserve it? How did it make you feel?

_____

_____

_____

_____

_____

▶ How does knowing God had a plan to save you even before you were born shape your view of His love?

_____

_____

_____

_____

_____

▶ When you mess up, do you run from God or to Him? How can you remind yourself that His love is always there?

_____

_____

_____

_____

_____

Day 3

A Promise That Stands

"I set My rainbow in the cloud, and it shall be for the sign of the covenant between Me and the earth." Genesis 9:13-16

- God shows His love through the promise of never flooding the earth again.

Devotional Illustration

Imagine a time when someone made a promise to you—maybe a friend said they had your back, a mentor assured you they'd support you, or a family member reminded you that they'd always be there. A real promise, when kept, brings peace. It makes you feel secure, knowing that no matter what happens, you can count on that word.

After the flood, God placed a rainbow in the sky as a sign of His promise never to destroy the earth with water again. This wasn't just a random display of colors—it was a symbol of His love and faithfulness. Every time a storm passes and the sun shines through, that rainbow is a reminder that God keeps His word.

Life comes with storms. You might face struggles—financial stress, broken relationships, or feeling like you're not where you should be. But just like the rainbow follows the storm, God's love is always present. His promises stand, no matter how dark things seem. He won't leave you; He won't give up on you, and He won't break His word.

The next time you see a rainbow, remember this: God's love is constant. His promises are real. You can trust Him to see you through the storm and bring you into the light.

Prayer

Father, thank You for being a God who keeps His promises. When life feels uncertain, help me to trust in Your love and faithfulness. Remind me that after every storm, Your light shines through. Let me rest in the truth that Your love never fails. In Jesus' name, Amen.

Affirmations

1. God's promises for my life are true and unshakable.
2. His love shines even after life's storms.
3. I trust in God's faithfulness, knowing He will never leave me.
4. The rainbow is my reminder that God's love is everlasting.
5. No matter what I face, I am covered by God's promises.

Anchor Thought: God's promises never fail—His covenant is unbreakable.

Reflection Questions

▶ Have you ever doubted God's promises in tough times? How did He show you He was still there?

_____

_____

_____

_____

_____

▶ What are some promises in the Bible that remind you of God's love and faithfulness?

_____

_____

_____

_____

_____

▶ How can you hold on to God's promises when life gets challenging?

_____

_____

_____

_____

_____

Day 4

God's Love is Steadfast and Faithful

"And the Lord passed before him and proclaimed, 'The Lord, the Lord God, merciful and gracious, long-suffering, and abounding in goodness and truth." Exodus 34:6

- God's love is merciful, patient, and full of goodness.

Devotional Illustration

Think about a time when someone made a promise to you and kept it—maybe a friend who showed up when they said they would or a family member who supported you no matter what. Their consistency and faithfulness made you feel secure, like you could trust them completely. But on the flip side, when someone breaks a promise, it hurts. It can make you question if you can really count on them.

Now, think about God. Exodus 34:6 says, *"The Lord, the Lord, the compassionate and gracious God, slow to anger, abounding in love and faithfulness."* Unlike people, God never breaks His promises. His love isn't temporary or based on how well we perform. It doesn't change depending on the situation. God's love is **steadfast**—it holds firm no matter what. His faithfulness means He will always be there, always keep His word, and always love you, even when you mess up.

God isn't like the people in your life who may let you down. He is **abounding** in love, which means His love overflows—it's more than enough. He doesn't run out of patience with you. Even when you struggle, even when you don't feel worthy, His love remains constant. So, no matter what's happening in your life, you can always count on God's love to hold you up.

Prayer

Lord, thank You for being a God of compassion and faithfulness. Even when I struggle, You never leave me. Your love is abounding and unchanging. Help me to trust in Your promises and reflect Your love in my daily life. In Jesus' name, Amen.

Affirmations

1. God's love for me is steadfast and never fails.
2. God is faithful to His promises, and I can always trust Him.
3. Even when I fall short, God's love for me remains the same.
4. I am surrounded by God's abounding love every day.
5. I choose to walk in confidence, knowing that God is always with me.

Anchor Thought: God's love is full of mercy, grace, and truth—unchanging through time.

Reflection Questions

▶ How does knowing that God's love is steadfast and faithful change the way you see Him?

_____

_____

_____

_____

_____

▶ Have you ever felt like God was far away? How does Exodus 34:6 remind you of His closeness and love?

_____

_____

_____

_____

_____

▶ How can you reflect God's steadfast love to the people around you?

_____

_____

_____

_____

_____

Faithful Through Every Season

"Therefore know that the Lord your God, He is God, the faithful God who keeps covenant and mercy for a thousand generations with those who love Him and keep His commandments." Deuteronomy 7:9

- God's love is faithful, enduring through generations.

Devotional Illustration

Think about someone who has always been there for you. Maybe it's a parent who never lets you down, a friend who has your back no matter what, or a mentor who believes in you when you don't believe in yourself. Their consistency and loyalty make you feel secure, knowing you can count on them, no matter what.

Now, imagine that kind of loyalty multiplied beyond anything you can imagine. That's what God's faithfulness is like. In Deuteronomy 7:9, we're reminded that God keeps His promises and shows mercy for a thousand generations. His love didn't just begin with you; it's been there all through history, reaching across time to embrace you now.

People change. Circumstances shift. Friends might let you down. But God? He never changes. His love isn't temporary or based on conditions—it's solid, steady, and eternal. Even when you mess up, He doesn't walk away. His faithfulness isn't based on how perfect you are, but on who He is.

When life feels uncertain, remember that God isn't going anywhere. His love is the rock you can stand on. The same God who was faithful to those before you is the same God who is faithful to you today.

Prayer

Lord, thank You for being faithful through every season of my life. Even when things change and people fail, You remain constant. Help me to trust Your love, even when I don't understand what's happening. Remind me that Your promises never fail and that You are always with me. In Jesus' name. Amen.

Affirmations

1. God's love for me is unshakable and never-ending.
2. I can trust God's faithfulness in every season of my life.
3. Even when things change, God remains the same.
4. God's promises are true for me, just as they were for generations before.
5. I am never alone because God is always with me.

Anchor Thought: God's faithfulness covers me—and generations after me.

Reflection Questions

▶ Have you ever experienced someone's loyalty and faithfulness? How did that make you feel?

_____

_____

_____

_____

_____

▶ How does knowing that God's love is unshakable give you confidence in your life today?

_____

_____

_____

_____

_____

▶ What are some ways you can trust God more in uncertain times?

_____

_____

_____

_____

_____

God Is Always With You

"*Be strong and of good courage, do not fear nor be afraid of them; for the Lord your God, He is the One who goes with you. He will not leave you nor forsake you.*"
Deuteronomy 31:6

- God's love assures us He is always with us.

Devotional Illustration

There are moments when life feels overwhelming. Maybe you're facing a major decision, dealing with tough challenges at work or school, or battling something personal that feels too big to handle. In those moments, it's easy to ask, "Where is God in all of this?" When things get difficult, it can feel like you're all alone, but the truth is that God is right there with you, even when you can't see or feel His presence.

Deuteronomy 31:6 reminds us that God will never leave us. He tells us to be strong and courageous because He is with us every step of the way. Imagine walking through a dark alley at night, unsure and afraid of what might happen. Now, picture having a strong, trusted friend with you, guiding you through the darkness. That friend's presence would give you courage and comfort, knowing you weren't walking alone.

God's love is like that. His presence is constant and unchanging. He walks with you through every challenge, every struggle, and every moment of fear. His love doesn't leave you when times get tough. Instead, it gives you the strength to keep moving forward, knowing that you are never by yourself. No matter what you're facing, God is right there beside you, holding you up.

Prayer

Lord, thank You for Your promise to never leave or forsake me. Help me to remember Your presence when fear tries to take over. Strengthen me with Your love so I can be courageous, knowing You are always by my side. In Jesus' name. Amen.

Affirmations

1. I am never alone because God is always with me.
2. God's love gives me the strength and courage to face any challenge.
3. I choose to walk in confidence, knowing God will never forsake me.
4. I trust God's love and presence to guide me through difficult times.
5. God's love surrounds me and gives me peace in every moment.

Anchor Thought: I walk in courage, knowing God never leaves my side.

Reflection Questions

▶ When you think of God's constant presence, how does it change the way you approach your fears or challenges?

_____

_____

_____

_____

_____

▶ Can you recall a time when you felt God's presence with you, even if you didn't recognize it right away?

_____

_____

_____

_____

_____

▶ How can knowing that God will never leave you give you peace in the middle of struggles?

_____

_____

_____

_____

_____

Love That Never Runs Out

"Oh, give thanks to the Lord, for He is good! For His mercy endures forever." Psalm 136:1

- God's love is shown in His goodness and never-ending mercy.

Devotional Illustration

Have you ever had a friend who always shows up for you? No matter the situation, they're always there to support you, even when you make mistakes. It feels incredible to know someone has your back, but even the most loyal friend can get tired, frustrated, or overwhelmed. Eventually, they might reach their limit and not be able to give as much as they once did.

But God's love isn't like that. Psalm 136:1 reminds us that His mercy endures forever. This means God's love and mercy never run out. He's not going to get tired of forgiving you or stop showing up for you when you need Him. His goodness isn't based on how perfect you are, but on who He is. Every day, He wakes you up, provides for you, and covers you with His grace, no matter how your past day looked.

Think about that for a moment—no matter where you've been, no matter what you've done, God's love is always there, steady and unwavering. When people disappoint you or let you down, He's still there. When you feel unworthy of a second chance, He offers it freely. His love isn't earned—it's given freely, day after day. That's the beauty of God's love: it never stops, it never runs out, and it's always there, no matter what.

Prayer

Lord, thank You for Your never-ending mercy. Even when I fall short, Your love remains. Help me to trust in Your goodness and remember that You are always there for me. Teach me to extend that same mercy to others. Let my life be a reflection of Your unfailing love. In Jesus' name. Amen.

Affirmations

1. God's love for me never runs out—His mercy endures forever.
2. No mistake can separate me from the goodness of God.
3. I am covered by grace and surrounded by His love.
4. Even when people fail me, God remains faithful.
5. I choose to show mercy because God has shown me mercy.

Anchor Thought: God's mercy is endless—His love never runs dry.

Reflection Questions

▶ How have you experienced God's mercy in your life? Can you think of a time when He gave you another chance?

_____

_____

_____

_____

_____

▶ How does knowing God's love never runs out help you when you feel distant from Him?

_____

_____

_____

_____

_____

▶ How can knowing that God will never leave you give you peace in the middle of struggles?

_____

_____

_____

_____

_____

A Love That Gives Second Chances

"The Lord is merciful and gracious, slow to anger, and abounding in mercy." Psalm 103:8

- God's love is full of mercy and grace, slow to anger.

Devotional Illustration

Think about a time when you really messed up—maybe you said something out of anger, hurt someone you care about, or made a choice you wish you could take back. It's hard when people look at your mistakes and make you feel like you'll never get it right. Sometimes, people hold grudges or cut you off. But here's the good news: God is not like that at all.

The Bible tells us in Psalm 103:8, that God is "compassionate and gracious, slow to anger, abounding in love." That means even when you fall short, God's love remains steady. He's not waiting to punish you or push you away. Instead, He's standing with open arms, ready to forgive and help you grow.

Mercy means God holds back the punishment we deserve, and grace means He gives us blessings we didn't earn. That's powerful. You might feel like you've gone too far or messed up too many times, but God's love is bigger than any failure. He sees your potential, even when you can't.

This doesn't mean we should keep doing wrong just because we know God will forgive us. His love should pull us closer, making us want to live better. Every time you turn back to God, He's ready to give you a fresh start. His love isn't about keeping score—it's about staying connected to you, no matter what. Today, remember: God's love never quits on you.

Prayer

Lord, thank You for being merciful and gracious toward me. Even when I mess up, You remain patient and kind. Help me to trust in Your love and to extend that same grace to others, offering second chances as You have done for me. In Jesus' name. Amen.

Affirmations

1. God is merciful and patient with me.
2. I am loved, even when I fail.
3. God's grace gives me the strength to keep going.
4. I will be slow to anger and quick to forgive.
5. God's love for me is unshakable.

Anchor Thought: God's grace rewrites my story with second chances.

Reflection Questions

▶ How does it feel to know that God is slow to anger and full of mercy toward you?

_____

_____

_____

_____

_____

▶ Have you ever experienced a time when God gave you a second chance?

_____

_____

_____

_____

_____

▶ How can you reflect God's mercy by being more patient with others?

_____

_____

_____

_____

_____

A Love That Feels Your Pain

"The Lord is gracious and full of compassion, Slow to anger and great in mercy. The Lord is good to all, And His tender mercies are over all His works." Psalm 145:8-9

- God's love is compassionate and full of mercy.

Devotional Illustration

Have you ever felt like no one really gets what you're going through? Maybe you were dealing with pressure at work, school, or in your personal life, and even though people were around, it felt like no one truly understood. Then, out of nowhere, someone showed up and just listened. No lectures. No judging. They just sat with you, cared, and let you be real. That's what true compassion looks like.

God's love is like that, but even deeper. He's not far off, looking down from heaven without feeling what we feel. Psalm 86:15 says, *"But You, O Lord, are a God full of compassion, and gracious, long-suffering and abundant in mercy and truth."* That means God's heart is full of love and patience. When you're hurting, He's right there feeling it with you. When you're struggling to make it through the day, He sees you and cares deeply.

A lot of us grow up thinking God is just about rules and punishment, but that's not who He really is. God wants a relationship with you. His love is steady, even when we mess up. He doesn't turn His back on us when we fall. Instead, He reaches out with mercy and helps us get back up. His love never runs out, and His compassion never fails. Whatever you're facing today, remember: God's love is personal, powerful, and patient. He's with you, and He's not letting go.

Prayer

Lord, thank You for being full of compassion and mercy. You understand my struggles and feel my pain with me. Help me to trust in Your love, knowing that You are always present and ready to comfort me. Let Your compassion guide me to show kindness to others. In Jesus' name. Amen.

Affirmations

1. God's love for me is full of compassion.
2. I am never alone—God understands my struggles.
3. I will show mercy and kindness to others.
4. God's love is patient with me.
5. I trust in God's abundant mercy.

Anchor Thought: God feels what I feel—His compassion surrounds me.

Reflection Questions

▶ How does it change your perspective to know that God feels what you feel?

_____

_____

_____

_____

_____

▶ When has God's compassion comforted you in a tough time?

_____

_____

_____

_____

_____

▶ How can you be more compassionate toward others?

_____

_____

_____

_____

_____

A Love That Never Fades

"Can a woman forget her nursing child, and not have compassion on the son of her womb? Surely they may forget, yet I will not forget you. See, I have inscribed you on the palms of My hands; Your walls are continually before Me." Isaiah 49:15-16

- God's love is so strong that He will never forget us.

Devotional Illustration

Have you ever felt like you were left out or forgotten? Maybe your friends stopped checking in, or the people you thought had your back just disappeared. It can make you feel small, unimportant, and even invisible. That kind of loneliness is real, and it hurts. But here's the good news: God promises that He *never* forgets you.

Isaiah 49:15-16 gives us a beautiful picture of God's love. It says, *"Can a mother forget her nursing child? Can she feel no love for the child she has borne? But even if that were possible, I would not forget you! See, I have written your name on the palms of my hands."* Think about that for a second. A mother's love is supposed to be one of the strongest loves on earth, but God says His love goes even deeper. Your name—*your* life and story—are written right on His hands.

That means every time you feel invisible or unimportant, God is reminding you, "I see you. I love you. You matter to Me." His love doesn't fade away like people's attention sometimes does. His love is solid, permanent, and personal. No matter how many times you feel overlooked, God's eyes are always on you. You are *always* on His heart. Rest in that truth today: You are fully known, fully seen, and fully loved by God, and He's never letting you go.

Prayer

Lord, thank You for always remembering me. Even when I feel unseen, I know that You see me and that Your love for me is constant. Help me trust in Your promises and find peace knowing that I am never forgotten by You. In Jesus' name. Amen.

Affirmations

1. I am always on God's mind.
2. God's love for me never fades or weakens.
3. Even if people forget me, God never will.
4. I am permanently inscribed in God's hands.
5. I am deeply valued and treasured by God.

Anchor Thought: I am remembered, engraved on God's hands—never forgotten.

Reflection Questions

▶ Have you ever felt forgotten? How does it comfort you to know that God never forgets you?

_____

_____

_____

_____

_____

▶ What does it mean to you that your name is inscribed on God's hands?

_____

_____

_____

_____

▶ How can you remind yourself daily of God's unfailing love?

_____

_____

_____

_____

_____

A Love That Stands Firm

"For the mountains shall depart and the hills be removed, but My kindness shall not depart from you, nor shall My covenant of peace be removed," says the Lord, who has mercy on you." Isaiah 54:10

- God's love is unshakable; His kindness never leaves.

Devotional Illustration

Have you ever stood at the base of a huge mountain and just looked up in awe? Mountains seem unshakable, like they'll be standing tall forever. But the truth is, even mountains can change. Over time, storms, earthquakes, and erosion can break them down. What seems solid today can fall apart tomorrow.

But God's love? It's stronger than any mountain you've ever seen. Isaiah 54:10 says, *"Though the mountains be shaken and the hills be removed, yet my unfailing love for you will not be shaken nor my covenant of peace be removed."* That's a powerful promise. It means that even if everything around you falls apart—your job, your friendships, your plans—God's love for you remains solid and unchanging.

A lot of us put our trust in things that don't last. We chase success, money, and the approval of others, thinking those things will keep us secure. But all of that can fade or fall apart. God wants you to build your life on something stronger—His love. His love is steady, faithful, and always there, no matter what storms hit your life.

When life shakes you up—and it will—remember this: God's love is your firm foundation. You don't have to be afraid of losing it, because it's locked in forever. Stand strong, knowing you are deeply loved by a God who never changes and never lets go.

Prayer

Lord, thank You that Your love is unshakable. Even when everything around me changes, Your kindness remains. Help me to rely on Your unwavering love as my firm foundation. I trust in Your faithfulness, knowing that You will never leave me. In Jesus' name. Amen.

Affirmations

1. God's love for me never changes.
2. No matter what happens, I am secure in God's kindness.
3. I will not be shaken because I stand on God's promises.
4. My peace comes from God, not from the world.
5. I am safe in the unchanging love of my Father.

Anchor Thought: God's covenant love holds me steady, even in life's storms.

Reflection Questions

▶ What are some things in life that feel unshakable but really aren't?

_____

_____

_____

_____

_____

▶ How can you rely more on God's unchanging love instead of temporary things?

_____

_____

_____

_____

_____

▶ When has God's love carried you through a difficult season?

_____

_____

_____

_____

_____

Drawn by Everlasting Love

"Yes, I have loved you with an everlasting love; therefore with lovingkindness I have drawn you." Jeremiah 31:3

- God's love is eternal and draws us near to Him.

Devotional Illustration

Have you noticed how a lot of things in life don't last? Friendships can fade, money can run out, and even our feelings can change from one moment to the next. One day you're on top of the world, and the next you feel like everything is falling apart. But here's the truth you can hold onto: God's love *never* runs out.

Jeremiah 31:3 reminds us, *"I have loved you with an everlasting love; I have drawn you with unfailing kindness."* That means His love isn't temporary or based on how good we've been. It's eternal. No matter what's going on around you—or even inside you—God's love stays strong.

Think about a time when you felt far from God. Maybe you were too busy, frustrated, or made choices you regret. Even then, God didn't give up on you. He's always calling you back, not with guilt trips, but with grace. His love is like a deep well that never dries up, no matter how much you need.

We sometimes think we have to earn God's love or keep His approval by doing everything right. But that's not how His love works. God's love is built on *who He is*, not what we do. He loved you before you even knew Him, and He's going to keep loving you forever. So, take a deep breath today and rest in this truth: God's love for you is endless, and He's never letting you go.

Prayer

Lord, thank You for loving me with an everlasting love. No matter how far I go or what I face, Your love remains constant. Help me to rest in the security of Your unfailing love and draw closer to You each day. In Jesus' name. Amen.

Affirmations

1. God's love for me is everlasting.
2. Nothing can separate me from the love of God.
3. I am drawn to God by His kindness and grace.
4. I am loved deeply, no matter what I've done.
5. I will rest in the security of God's unchanging love.

Anchor Thought: God's love is eternal—He keeps drawing me near.

Reflection Questions

▶ How does knowing God's love is everlasting change the way you see yourself?

_____

_____

_____

_____

_____

▶ Have you ever felt God drawing you back to Him? What was that experience like?

_____

_____

_____

_____

_____

▶ What would it look like to rest in the security of God's love?

_____

_____

_____

_____

_____

Joy Is Coming

"For His anger is but for a moment, His favor is for life;
Weeping may endure for a night, But joy comes
in the morning." Psalm 30:5

- God's love renews us daily with His mercy and faithfulness.

Devotional Illustration

Have you ever had one of those nights where no matter how hard you tried, sleep just wouldn't come? Maybe your heart was heavy with stress, regret, or pain. It's crazy how the quiet of the night can make all your thoughts and worries feel even louder. Everything seems darker, and it can feel like you're all alone. But then, without fail, morning comes. The sky starts to brighten, and the sunlight sneaks through your blinds. Even if your problems haven't gone away, that sunrise reminds you: the night didn't last forever.

That's exactly what Psalm 30:5 tells us. It says, "Weeping may endure for a night, but joy comes in the morning." God understands that life gets heavy sometimes. We might cry, mess up, or feel like we're drowning in our struggles. But here's the good news—God's love is deeper than all of that. His correction might last for a moment, but His love, favor, and grace last a lifetime. That's real love.

Think about it: just like the sun rises every single day, God's love shows up for you over and over. His love brings fresh mercy, new strength, and a reason to keep going. No matter how long or dark your night feels, joy *will* come. Why? Because the God who loves you is always working behind the scenes, even when you can't see it yet. You're not forgotten, and you're not alone. God's love is making a way for your breakthrough. Hold on—your morning is coming.

Prayer

Lord, thank You that Your love renews me each day with Your mercy and faithfulness. Even in the darkest moments, You promise that joy will come in the morning. Help me trust You through difficult seasons, knowing that Your love will bring me through. In Jesus' name. Amen

Affirmations

1. God's love is constant, even when life feels dark.
2. Joy is coming, because my God never fails me.
3. Each morning brings fresh mercy and new hope.
4. I trust God's timing, even when the night feels long.
5. I am never alone—God is with me in the night and the morning.

Anchor Thought: God's love brings joy—even after my darkest nights.

Reflection Questions

▶ What does it mean to you that God's love offers you a clean slate, no matter how many times you've failed?

_____

_____

_____

_____

_____

▶ Can you think of a time when someone gave you a second chance? How did that change your relationship with them?

_____

_____

_____

_____

_____

▶ How can you practice giving second chances to others this week, reflecting God's mercy?

_____

_____

_____

_____

_____

Gentle Love, Strong Hands

"I drew them with gentle cords, with bands of love, and I was to them as those who take the yoke from their neck. I stooped and fed them." Hosea 11:4

- God's love is gentle and compassionate, drawing us to Him.

Devotional Illustration

Have you ever had a coach or mentor who knew exactly when to push you to do your best, but also when to step in with care and support? Maybe it's the coach who expects you to give your all on the court or field, but then takes the time to check in with you afterward to see if you're okay—emotionally, mentally, and physically. That balance of strength and kindness can make a huge impact. It shows you that they aren't just concerned with the result; they genuinely care about *you* as a person.

God's love is like that coach. Hosea 11:4 gives us a clear picture of how God interacts with us. He doesn't force us to follow Him or demand our love. Instead, He draws us in with cords of love. Imagine being gently pulled in by a rope of care, not pushed or dragged. His love is kind and patient, offering a safe space for us to grow.

When life gets tough, God sees our struggles and steps in with compassion. The verse says, "I stooped and fed them"—meaning God personally meets us where we are and provides what we need. He knows when we're exhausted, frustrated, or hurting, and He doesn't leave us to struggle alone. His love is powerful enough to lift the heavy burdens we carry, but it's also tender enough to care for our souls.

God's love is both strong and gentle. When you're tired or weighed down, remember that God's love is there to refresh and strengthen you. You don't have to carry your burdens alone—He's right there, ready to lift you up.

Prayer

Father, thank You for drawing me with love and for lifting the burdens I carry. Help me to feel Your gentle care every day. Remind me that You see my struggles and meet my needs with compassion. Teach me to trust Your loving hands. In Jesus' name. Amen.

Affirmations

1. God's love gently draws me closer every day.
2. The Lord lifts my burdens and gives me rest.
3. I am cared for by a compassionate and loving Father.
4. God meets my needs and refreshes my soul.
5. I am never alone—His love surrounds and strengthens me.

Anchor Thought: God lifts my burdens and feeds my soul with gentle love.

Reflection Questions

▶ What does it mean to you that God draws you with love rather than forcing you? How have you felt His gentle pull in your life?

_____

_____

_____

_____

_____

▶ Can you think of a time when you were weighed down and God stepped in to lift that burden? What did that experience teach you about His love?

_____

_____

_____

_____

_____

▶ How can remembering God's gentle and compassionate love change the way you handle stress or challenges this week? What's one burden you can trust Him to carry right now?

_____

_____

_____

_____

_____

Forgiven and Free

"Who is a God like You, pardoning iniquity and passing over the transgression of the remnant of His heritage? He does not retain His anger forever, because He delights in mercy." Micah 7:18

- God's love is forgiving, and He delights in showing mercy.

Devotional Illustration

Imagine carrying a heavy backpack filled with every wrong move you've ever made—bad decisions, broken trust, missed chances. That's what guilt can feel like. Maybe you've snapped at your mom, ghosted a friend, or made a choice you knew wasn't right. The weight of shame can pile up fast, and before you know it, you're dragging through life like you've got chains on your soul. The enemy wants you to believe that you'll always carry that weight, that you're stuck in your past. But God's love says something different.

Micah 7:18 says that God delights in showing mercy. That means He actually enjoys forgiving you. He's not sitting high and waiting to throw lightning bolts. He's standing with open arms, ready to take the weight off your shoulders. When you come to Him with a real heart and admit where you've messed up, He doesn't hesitate to forgive you. He wipes the slate clean. No hesitation. No holding it over your head.

God's love doesn't just forgive you—it frees you. He removes the backpack, breaks the chains, and reminds you that you are not your worst mistake. You are His son. You are loved, chosen, and accepted. God wants you walking in freedom, not shame. Each new day is a chance to move forward in grace, strength, and purpose. That's what His love does. That's what makes you forgiven *and* free.

Prayer

Father, thank You for loving me even when I mess up. Thank You for forgiving me and giving me a fresh start. Help me to see myself the way You see me—free, whole, and loved. Teach me to walk in that truth every day. In Jesus' name. Amen.

Affirmations

1. I am forgiven and free because of God's mercy.
2. God delights in showing me grace and love.
3. My past mistakes do not define my future.
4. Each day is a new start with God's mercy.
5. I will extend forgiveness to others as God forgives me.

Anchor Thought: God delights in forgiving me and setting me free.

Reflection Questions:

▶ What does it mean to you that God delights in showing you mercy?

_____

_____

_____

_____

_____

▶ Can you recall a time when you felt God's forgiveness lift a burden off your shoulders?

_____

_____

_____

_____

_____

▶ How can you practice showing mercy to someone else this week?

_____

_____

_____

_____

_____

Love God, Love Others

"Jesus said to him, 'You shall love the Lord your God with all your heart, with all your soul, and with all your mind.' This is the first and great commandment. And the second is like it: 'You shall love your neighbor as yourself." Matthew 22:37-39

- God teaches us to love Him and others with all our hearts.

Devotional Illustration

Think about the strongest team you've ever been part of—maybe it was a sports team, a school project group, or even your own family. On a real team, everyone brings something valuable to the table. You depend on each other. When one person is off, the whole team feels it. That's how God designed life to work—connected, united, and held together by love.

Jesus makes the command simple, but powerful: Love God first, and then love people. Not halfway. Not when it's convenient. But with all your heart, soul, and mind. That kind of love means putting God first in the way you think, speak, and live. It's not just about saying you love God—it's about showing it through your choices, your time, and your trust in Him every day.

From that place of loving God flows the ability to love others. And let's be real—that can be tough. People will test your patience, disrespect you, or ignore you. But God's love in you helps you forgive, show grace, and walk in peace. Loving others doesn't mean letting people treat you however they want—it means seeing them the way God sees them and choosing to respond with wisdom and kindness.

When you love God fully, it changes how you see yourself and how you show up in the world. It's not about being perfect. It's about choosing to grow in love—one day at a time, with God leading the way.

Prayer

Lord, help me to love You with all my heart, soul, and mind. Teach me to love others with kindness, patience, and grace, even when it's difficult. Show me how to reflect Your love in my daily life and be a witness of Your goodness to those around me. In Jesus' name. Amen.

Affirmations

1. I love God with all my heart, soul, and mind.
2. God's love fills me and helps me love others well.
3. I am a reflection of God's love in my community.
4. Loving others is part of my worship to God.
5. I choose love over anger, kindness over pride.

Anchor Thought: Loving God helps me love others well.

Reflection Questions:

▶ What does loving God with all your heart, soul, and mind look like in your daily life?

_____

_____

_____

_____

_____

▶ How have you seen your relationship with God impact how you treat others?

_____

_____

_____

_____

▶ What's one way you can show love to someone in need this week?

_____

_____

_____

_____

_____

The Greatest Gift

"For God so loved the world that He gave His only begotten Son, that whoever believes in Him should not perish but have everlasting life." John 3:16

- God's love is shown through the gift of Jesus for our salvation.

Devotional Illustration

Think back to a time when someone gave you something that truly caught you off guard—maybe a surprise birthday gift, a pair of sneakers you had been wanting for a long time, or a message of encouragement when you were feeling low. That feeling of being noticed, appreciated, and cared for? That's just a glimpse of the kind of love God has for you.

John 3:16 says, "For God so loved the world that He gave His only Son..." This wasn't just a kind gesture—it was the ultimate act of love. God didn't just say He loves you—He proved it. He gave Jesus, not because you were perfect or had everything together, but because He sees your true worth. He wants you to live free—not trapped by fear, guilt, or shame.

Jesus' death on the cross wasn't just a sacrifice; it was a rescue mission. He stepped in for you. Every sin, every regret, every heavy weight you've carried—He took it all so you could walk in freedom. That's real love, and it changes everything.

When you say yes to God's love, you receive a new identity. You're no longer defined by your past—you're chosen, forgiven, and accepted. This isn't about being religious or pretending to have it all together. It's about a real relationship with a God who never gives up on you. His love is for you—right here, right now. You just have to receive it.

Prayer

God, thank You for the greatest gift—Jesus. I am humbled by Your love and sacrifice for me. Help me to never take this gift for granted and to live with gratitude for what You have done. May Your love fill my heart, and may I share the hope of eternal life with those around me. In Jesus' name. Amen.

Affirmations

1. God's love gave me the gift of salvation.
2. Jesus' sacrifice shows how deeply I am loved.
3. I have eternal life because I believe in Jesus.
4. God's love gives my life purpose and hope.
5. I am grateful for the greatest gift of all—Jesus.

Anchor Thought: Jesus is the ultimate gift of love—sent just for me.

Reflection Questions:

▶ What does the gift of Jesus mean to you personally?

_____

_____

_____

_____

_____

▶ How has receiving God's love through Jesus changed your life?

_____

_____

_____

_____

_____

▶ How can you share the gift of God's love with someone else this week?

_____

_____

_____

_____

_____

The Greatest Love of All

"Greater love has no one than this, than to lay down one's life for his friends." John 15:13

- Jesus shows the greatest love by sacrificing His life for us.

Devotional Illustration

Picture this: someone you care about is facing serious danger. You have the chance to step in and save them—even if it means risking your own life. Would you do it? Your answer would probably depend on how much you love them.

That's the kind of love Jesus showed us.

In John 15:13, Jesus says, "Greater love has no one than this: to lay down one's life for one's friends." That's exactly what He did. He laid down His life—not just for people who had it all together, but for us, even in our mess. He saw our struggles, our sins, and our pain—and still chose the cross.

That's real love.

Jesus didn't die for you because you were perfect. He died for you because He saw your worth. You might not always feel valuable, especially in a world that may make you feel like you're not good enough. But Jesus sees you, knows you, and still says, "You're worth dying for."

That kind of love changes everything. It gives you identity. It gives you strength. It gives you purpose.

You are not forgotten. You are not overlooked. You are deeply loved—by the One who gave everything to save you.

Let that truth settle in your heart today. Let it shape how you walk, how you think, and how you live. Jesus didn't just tell you you're loved—He proved it.

Prayer

Jesus, thank You for the greatest love that led You to lay down Your life for me. Help me to understand the depth of Your sacrifice and to live in the light of that love every day. Teach me to love others with the same selflessness and commitment that You showed me. In Jesus' name. Amen.

Affirmations

1. Jesus calls me His friend and proved His love by dying for me.
2. I am deeply loved and valued by God.
3. True love is selfless, and I choose to love others that way.
4. I am reminded daily of Christ's sacrifice and what it means for my life.
5. Nothing can compare to the love Jesus has shown me.

Anchor Thought: Jesus proved His love when He gave His life for me.

Reflection Questions

▶ What does it mean to you that Jesus calls you His friend and died for you?

_____

_____

_____

_____

_____

▶ How does knowing the depth of Jesus' sacrifice shape the way you view yourself?

_____

_____

_____

_____

▶ In what ways can you show selfless love to others this week, following Jesus' example?

_____

_____

_____

_____

_____

Loved Even When We Mess Up

"But God demonstrates His own love toward us, in that while we were still sinners, Christ died for us." Romans 5:8

- God's love is shown through Christ's death for us, even while we were sinners.

Devotional Illustration

Have you ever messed up so badly that you thought you couldn't bounce back? Maybe you broke a promise, failed at something important, or hurt someone you care about. It's easy to believe that love disappears when we fall short—but that's not how God loves.

Romans 5:8 says, "But God proves His own love for us in that while we were still sinners, Christ died for us." That means God didn't wait for us to clean ourselves up. He loved us right in the middle of the mess. His love came before the apology. Before the change. Before we even knew we needed saving.

That kind of love is deep. It's not earned by how good we are—it's rooted in who God is. His love is strong and steady. It doesn't turn away when things get hard or when we struggle. It stays. It forgives. It covers us when we feel ashamed, broken, or lost.

God's love frees us from pretending to have it all together. You don't have to fake it with Him. You can be real about where you are and still be completely loved and accepted. Every single day.

So, if you're carrying guilt, shame, or regret, bring it to God. His love is greater than your worst day, and He's not walking away from you. He's walking with you, ready to help you start fresh.

Prayer

Father, thank You for loving me even when I mess up. I am amazed by Your grace and mercy that never leaves me, no matter my failures. Help me to embrace Your forgiveness and extend the same love and grace to others. In Jesus' name. Amen.

Affirmations

1. God loves me unconditionally, even when I fail.
2. I am forgiven and free because of Jesus' sacrifice.
3. My worth is not based on my mistakes but on God's love.
4. I walk in grace and let go of guilt and shame.
5. God's love never changes, no matter what.

Anchor Thought: God's love met me in my mess and saved me anyway.

Reflection Questions

▶ Can you think of a time when you felt unworthy of God's love? How did He show you otherwise?

_____

_____

_____

_____

_____

▶ What's one area where you need to accept God's forgiveness and grace right now?

_____

_____

_____

_____

▶ How can you extend that same kind of grace to someone else this week?

_____

_____

_____

_____

_____

Nothing Can Separate Us

"Nor height nor depth, nor any other created thing, shall be able to separate us from the love of God which is in Christ Jesus our Lord." Romans 8:39

- Nothing can separate us from God's love in Christ.

Devotional Illustration

Have you ever had a friend move away or lost touch with someone you were once close to? Maybe time, distance, or disagreements got in the way. It can feel lonely when someone who mattered disappears from your life, leaving a space that's hard to fill. Sometimes, it even makes you question if relationships are worth the risk.

But God's love is different. Romans 8:39 reminds us that *nothing* can separate us from His love—not distance, not mistakes, not failure, not even the toughest storms. His love is unbreakable. It's the kind of love that stays close, even when everything else feels distant or uncertain.

Life isn't always easy. You might go through seasons where you feel far from God, where doubts, disappointments, or hard times make you wonder if He's still there. But His love never changes. It meets you in your lowest moments and walks with you through your highs. His love doesn't give up when you mess up. It keeps reaching, keeps holding, and keeps showing up.

Even when you feel alone or unsure, God hasn't left you. His love surrounds you—even when you don't feel it. You're never out of His reach.

So, when life feels shaky, when people walk away, or when you feel like you don't have it all together, remember this: God's love is the one thing that never breaks, never leaves, and never stops. You are deeply loved, completely seen, and fully known—always.

Prayer

Lord, thank You that nothing can separate me from Your love. Even when life feels shaky or I feel far from You, You never leave me. Help me to trust Your unchanging love, stand strong in it, and walk in it every day. In Jesus' name. Amen.

Affirmations

1. God's love is unbreakable and constant.
2. No challenge or mistake can separate me from His love.
3. I am held securely in Christ's love every moment.
4. I trust God's love to carry me through every season.
5. God is always with me—His love never fails.

Anchor Thought: I am inseparable from God's love—it reaches me wherever I am.

Reflection Questions

▶ When have you felt distant from God? How did you realize He was still with you?

_____

_____

_____

_____

_____

▶ What situations make you question God's love, and how can you remind yourself of His promises?

_____

_____

_____

_____

_____

▶ How does knowing God's love is unbreakable give you strength in hard times?

_____

_____

_____

_____

_____

Love That Gives Life

"In this the love of God was manifested toward us, that God has sent His only begotten Son into the world, that we might live through Him. In this is love, not that we loved God, but that He loved us and sent His Son to be the propitiation for our sins." 1 John 4:9-10

- God's love is revealed in the sacrifice of Jesus for our sins.

Devotional Illustration

Sometimes we think love is just about feelings or sweet words. But real love goes way deeper—it's about action and sacrifice. Think about someone giving up something huge just so you could have a better life. That kind of love leaves a mark. It changes how you see yourself and how you live.

1 John 4:9-10 shows us what real love looks like. It says God loved us so much that He sent His only Son into the world—not just to be near us, but to *give His life* for us. Jesus carried all of our mistakes, shame, guilt, and pain—things we couldn't fix on our own. He stepped in, took our place, and made a way for us to live with purpose and freedom.

What's wild is that God did this *before* we ever thought about loving Him back. He didn't wait for us to get it together. His love made the first move. And it wasn't passive—it was powerful. It heals, saves, and lifts us up when we feel low.

So, whenever you feel like you don't measure up, or like you've messed up too much, remember the cross. That's your proof that you're not forgotten. You are fully accepted and deeply loved.

God's love didn't just rescue you—it gave you a new start and a new reason to live. Every day, that love is calling you higher. All you have to do is say "yes."

Prayer

Father, thank You for loving me first and showing that love through Jesus. Your love gives me new life, purpose, and hope. Help me live each day remembering what You've done for me. Let Your love shape my choices and guide my steps. In Jesus' name. Amen.

Affirmations

1. God's love gave me new life through Jesus.
2. I am fully accepted and deeply loved by God.
3. My life has purpose because of God's sacrifice.
4. I live in freedom, knowing Jesus paid the price.
5. God's love is the foundation of my hope and peace.

Anchor Thought: Jesus is the proof that God's love brings life.

Reflection Questions

▶ What does it mean to you that God made the first move in loving you?

_____

_____

_____

_____

_____

▶ How has Jesus' sacrifice changed the way you live your life?

_____

_____

_____

_____

_____

▶ In what ways can you share God's life-giving love with others this week?

_____

_____

_____

_____

_____

Staying Close to the Source

"And we have known and believed the love that God has for us. God is love, and he who abides in love abides in God, and God in him." 1 John 4:16

- God is Love, and we experience His love more deeply when we stay close to Him.

Devotional Illustration

Imagine your phone is on 1% battery, and you're nowhere near a charger. The stress kicks in, especially if you need it for GPS, music, or an important call. In the same way, when we drift too far from God, our spiritual battery runs low. The longer we stay disconnected from Him, the more drained and weak we feel—mentally, emotionally, and spiritually.

The Bible gives us hope in 1 John 4:16, which says, "God is love." That means love isn't just something God has; it's who He is. When we stay connected to God, we stay connected to the source of all love, strength, and peace. Being close to Him—through prayer, reading the Bible, worship, or just quiet time—is like plugging into a charger. It refills us with a kind of love that the world can never give.

You don't have to work to earn God's love or chase after it; it's already yours because He loves you deeply and unconditionally. But you do have to choose to stay close. Think about staying within range of a Wi-Fi signal: the closer you are to the router, the stronger your connection. If you walk away, the signal weakens or cuts off completely.

Don't let distractions, doubts, or busyness pull you away from God's love. It's real, powerful, and always available to you. So, abide in it daily. Live in that love. Let it fill your heart and soul, and you will find strength to face every day.

Prayer

Father, thank You for being Love—unfailing, endless, and true. Please help me stay close to You every day and remain filled with Your perfect love. Let Your presence surround me with peace and power, no matter what challenges come my way. I desire to abide in You always. In Jesus' name, amen.

Affirmations

1. God's love lives in me because I live in Him.
2. I stay connected to my Source—God's love never runs out.
3. I am never alone; God's presence surrounds me.
4. I walk in love because I walk with God.
5. Love is my foundation, my fuel, and my focus.

Anchor Thought: When I stay close to God, I stay full of His love.

Reflection Questions

▶ What does it look like for you to "abide" in God's love during a regular day?

_____

_____

_____

_____

_____

▶ When do you feel your spiritual battery running low?

_____

_____

_____

_____

▶ What's one way you can stay more connected to God's love this week?

_____

_____

_____

_____

_____

Day 23

God Loved You First

"We love Him because He first loved us." 1 John 4:19

- Our love for God is a response to His first love for us.

Devotional Illustration

Remember the first time someone did something kind for you before you even asked? Maybe a friend picked up the tab when you were low on cash. Maybe a coach, teacher, or mentor spoke life into you at a moment when you felt invisible. It probably caught you off guard—but in the best way. And it likely made you want to say thank you, return the favor, or at least never forget it.

That's how God's love works. The Bible says in 1 John 4:19, "We love because He first loved us." Think about that. Before you ever thought about God, He already had you on His mind. Before you ever prayed or went to church, God was loving you. Even when you were ignoring Him or running the other way, He still chose to love you. He sent Jesus to take your place, to forgive your sins, and to offer you new life—before you could do anything to deserve it.

That's real love. Not based on how good you are. Not based on how much you get right. It's based on who God is—**He is love** (1 John 4:16).

And when you realize how deep that love runs, it changes how you respond. You don't love God to earn anything. You love Him back because you're grateful. You walk with Him because He walked toward you first. Every prayer, every "yes," every step of obedience is your way of saying, "Thank You."

That's the power of love that goes first.

Prayer

Lord, thank You for loving me first, even before I knew You or deserved it. Help me to love You back with all my heart, soul, and mind. May my life be a constant and joyful response to Your amazing, unfailing love. In Jesus' name, amen.

Affirmations

1. God loved me before I knew Him.
2. I respond to God's love with faith and obedience.
3. I don't have to earn God's love—it's already mine.
4. My love for God grows stronger every day.
5. I live as someone deeply loved by the Father.

Anchor Thought: God made the first move—my love is a response to His.

Reflection Questions

▶ How does knowing God loved you first change the way you see Him?

_____

_____

_____

_____

_____

▶ What are some ways you can show love back to God in your daily life?

_____

_____

_____

_____

▶ Are there any lies you've believed about having to earn God's love?

_____

_____

_____

_____

_____

From Dead Ends to
New Beginnings

"But God, who is rich in mercy, because of His great love with which He loved us, even when we were dead in trespasses, made us alive together with Christ (by grace you have been saved)." Ephesians 2:4-5

- God's love gives us new life, even when we are lost in sin.

Devotional Illustration

Ever felt stuck in a place you didn't think you could come back from? Maybe you messed up big time—hurt someone, lost control, made bad choices, or just felt like life hit a wall you couldn't climb over. It's easy to believe that you're too far gone or too broken to fix. But the truth is, God's love can reach you even there—especially there.

Ephesians 2:4-5 says that even when we were "dead in sin," God made us alive in Christ. That means when you were at your lowest, when you felt the most unworthy, God didn't turn away—He stepped in. He didn't wait for you to get it all together. He moved toward you with **mercy** and **love** that's deeper than anything you've ever experienced. His mercy isn't limited. His love isn't small. You didn't earn a second chance—grace gave it to you.

New life is real and possible. It's not just a future hope; it's something you can walk in right now. A new way of thinking. A new direction. A new identity that's not chained to your past. You don't have to stay buried in shame, guilt, or regret.

2 Corinthians 5:17 says, "If anyone is in Christ, he is a new creation." That includes you. Your past doesn't get the final say. God's love rewrites the story. His love restores what was broken and gives you power to move forward—whole, healed, and made new in Him.

Prayer

Father, thank You for loving me even when I was at my lowest and feeling lost. Thank You for making me alive again through Jesus Christ. Help me to walk in this new life every day with joy, confidence, and hope, trusting fully in Your grace and power. In Jesus' name. Amen.

Affirmations

1. I have been made alive in Christ.
2. God's mercy covers my past.
3. I walk in new life, not shame.
4. Grace found me and gave me a future.
5. I am not defined by my mistakes—I'm defined by God's love.

Anchor Thought: God's love revives dead places and gives me a fresh start.

Reflection Questions

▶ When have you felt like you hit a dead end? How does this verse give you hope?

_____

_____

_____

_____

_____

▶ What does it mean to you to be "made alive" in Christ?

_____

_____

_____

_____

▶ What old labels or thoughts do you need to leave behind?

_____

_____

_____

_____

Deeper Than You Think

"That Christ may dwell in your hearts through faith; that you, being rooted and grounded in love, may be able to comprehend with all the saints what is the width and length and depth and height— to know the love of Christ which passes knowledge; that you may be filled with all the fullness of God." Ephesians 3:17-19

- God's love for us is vast and beyond full understanding.

Devotional Illustration

Imagine standing at the edge of the ocean. You see waves crashing and the horizon stretching out far in front of you. It's beautiful, powerful, and peaceful all at once. But you also know—that's just the surface. Beneath those waves is a whole world: deep waters, strong currents, hidden treasures, and mystery.

That's kind of how God's love is. You can feel it, know it, and even experience it—but you'll never reach the bottom. Ephesians 3:18-19 says God's love is wide, long, high, and deep. Paul even says it "surpasses knowledge." In other words, it's too big to fully understand, but God still invites us to explore it. And the more you grow in that love, the more grounded your life becomes.

Being rooted in God's love means you're not easily shaken. When people talk down on you, when life gets rough, or when you mess up—you don't fall apart. You're planted in something stronger than opinions or mistakes. You know who you are and whose you are. That kind of love gives you stability and confidence.

God's love isn't just a good feeling you get during worship or prayer. It's a foundation. Something you can stand on, build on, and rely on. The deeper your roots grow in His love, the stronger and more peaceful your life becomes.

Don't just stand at the edge. Step in. Go deeper. Let God's love hold you, guide you, and change you from the inside out.

Prayer

Lord, help me to be deeply rooted and grounded in Your amazing love. Even when I don't fully understand it, I choose to trust and believe in its power. Fill me completely with Your love so that it overflows in every part of my life. In Jesus' name, amen.

Affirmations

1. God's love is the foundation of my life.
2. I am rooted and grounded in God's truth.
3. God's love for me is bigger than I can imagine.
4. I am secure in who I am in Christ.
5. My life is filled with the fullness of God.

Anchor Thought: God's love is deeper than I know—and it holds me steady.

Reflection Questions

▶ What helps you stay grounded in God's love when life feels unstable?

_____

_____

_____

_____

_____

▶ Can you think of a time when God's love surprised you or went deeper than you expected?

_____

_____

_____

_____

_____

▶ What does it look like to build your life on the foundation of love?

_____

_____

_____

_____

_____

Love That Learns

"And this I pray, that your love may abound still more and more in knowledge and all discernment." Philippians 1:9

- God's love leads us to grow in understanding and wisdom.

Devotional Illustration

Think about learning how to drive. At first, you're just trying not to mess up—keep it between the lines, don't hit anything, don't stall out, and definitely don't panic. Your main focus is survival. But over time, with practice and experience, you get better. You learn how to read signs, recognize traffic patterns, and make smoother decisions. You go from surviving to driving with confidence and purpose.

That's exactly what happens when you grow in God's love. At first, it might feel like you're just trying to "do right" and not mess up. But God's love isn't about being perfect—it's about growing. Philippians 1:9 says, "I pray that your love may abound more and more in knowledge and depth of insight." That means your love isn't just supposed to feel good—it should also get smarter and stronger.

Real love isn't blind. Real love sees clearly. It knows when to speak up and when to stay silent. It helps you avoid traps, recognize truth, and respond with grace. The more time you spend with God—through prayer, the Word, and listening to the Holy Spirit—the more your love matures.

You'll start making better decisions—not just for yourself, but in how you treat others. You'll start to love like Jesus—strong, wise, patient, and full of grace.

So don't settle for shallow love. Ask God to help your love grow deeper and wiser every day. Let His love guide your choices, sharpen your vision, and lead your life.

Prayer

God, help me grow deeper in love and wisdom each day. Fill my heart with kindness and my mind with understanding. Teach me to love others in a way that honors You and brings light to their lives. Guide me to reflect Your goodness always. In Jesus' name, amen.

Affirmations

1. My love grows deeper and wiser every day.
2. God teaches me how to love with truth and grace.
3. I walk in discernment guided by love.
4. My choices reflect God's wisdom.
5. I grow in understanding through God's Spirit.

Anchor Thought: Love grows when guided by wisdom and truth.

Reflection Questions

▶ What's one way God's love has helped you grow in wisdom?

_____

_____

_____

_____

_____

▶ How can you be more intentional in showing wise love to others?

_____

_____

_____

_____

_____

▶ What do you think it means to have love that "abounds more and more"?

_____

_____

_____

_____

_____

Loving Discipline

"For whom the Lord loves He chastens, and scourges every son whom He receives." Hebrews 12:6

- God's love corrects and disciplines us for our good.

Devotional Illustration

Ever had someone call you out—not to embarrass you, but because they actually cared about you? Maybe it was a coach who saw your potential and pushed you to go harder. Or maybe a mentor pulled you aside and told you to check your attitude. It probably didn't feel great at the time. You might've even been annoyed or defensive. But deep down, you knew it came from a place of love and belief in who you could become.

That's how God's discipline works. Hebrews 12:6 says, "The Lord disciplines the one He loves." He's not out to hurt you or shame you. He's guiding you like a good Father. He sees the whole picture—your past, your present, and your future. He knows what you need to grow, even when you don't.

God's discipline can come through conviction, correction, or a closed door. It may feel uncomfortable in the moment, but it always has a purpose. Just like a good trainer pushes your body to get stronger, God stretches your heart and character so you can mature. He wants you to walk in wisdom, strength, and freedom.

So, if God is checking your spirit or redirecting your steps, don't run from it. Don't shut down. Lean in. Let Him teach you. Trust that His correction is love in action—proof that you're His and He's invested in your growth.

Discipline may feel tough now, but it leads to something greater: a life that honors God and reflects His heart.

Prayer

Father, thank You for loving me enough to correct and guide me. Help me to receive Your discipline with a humble and open heart. I trust that You are shaping and molding me for good, so I can grow stronger in faith and character. In Jesus' name, amen.

Affirmations

1. God corrects me because He loves me.
2. Discipline is part of my growth.
3. I welcome God's guidance in every area.
4. I am maturing in faith through correction.
5. I am a beloved son, trained in love.

Anchor Thought: God's correction is proof of His love—it shapes me for His purpose.

Reflection Questions

▶ How have you experienced God's loving correction in your life?

_____

_____

_____

_____

_____

▶ What's the difference between punishment and discipline?

_____

_____

_____

_____

▶ How can you respond better to God's guidance?

_____

_____

_____

_____

_____

Clean for Real

"And from Jesus Christ, the faithful witness, the firstborn from the dead, and the ruler over the kings of the earth. To Him who loved us and washed us from our sins in His own blood." Revelation 1:5

- Jesus shows His love by washing us clean from sin with His blood.

Devotional Illustration

Imagine trying to clean a white shirt stained with something deep—like oil, ink, or grape juice. No matter how many times you scrub, soak, or wash it, the stain doesn't go away. It might fade a little, but it's still there. That's what sin is like. It leaves a mark that we just can't remove on our own, no matter how hard we try.

But there's good news. Revelation 1:5 says that Jesus loves us and has washed us from our sins—not with water or soap, but with His own blood. That might sound a little intense, but it's one of the most powerful truths in the Bible. His blood paid the full price for every sin, every mistake, and every mess. When Jesus died on the cross and rose again, He made a way for us to be completely clean—spiritually clean.

That means your past doesn't get the final word. The guilt you've been carrying? The shame that weighs you down? It doesn't stick anymore. If you've said yes to Jesus, you've been forgiven and made new. You're not walking around with a permanent stain. You're walking in freedom, grace, and a fresh start.

So don't let the enemy lie to you and say you're still dirty. You're not. You've been washed. God sees you as clean, whole, and deeply loved. So, lift your head, stand tall, and walk like someone who's been made new—because you have.

Prayer

Lord, thank You for loving me unconditionally and washing me clean from all my sins. Help me to live free from shame and guilt, fully knowing that I am forgiven. I gladly receive Your perfect love and choose to walk each day in Your amazing grace. In Jesus' name. Amen.

Affirmations

1. I am clean because of Jesus' love.
2. My past does not define my future.
3. I walk in freedom and forgiveness.
4. Jesus' blood has washed away every sin.
5. I live with confidence because I am loved and forgiven.

Anchor Thought: Because of Jesus, I am clean, loved, and made new.

Reflection Questions

▶ What does it mean to you to be "washed" by Jesus?

_____

_____

_____

_____

_____

▶ Are you holding onto guilt that Jesus already removed?

_____

_____

_____

_____

_____

▶ How can you live differently knowing you are truly forgiven?

_____

_____

_____

_____

_____

Appendix
Suggested Reading List

For Deeper Intimacy, Healing, and Identity in the Love of God

Devotionals & Daily Walk
- Jesus Calling – Sarah Young
- My Utmost for His Highest – Oswald Chambers
- New Morning Mercies – Paul David Tripp
- Reclaiming the Lost Art of Biblical Meditation – Robert J. Morgan

Identity & the Father's Love
- Abba's Child – Brennan Manning
- The Ragamuffin Gospel – Brennan Manning
- You Are the Beloved – Henri J.M. Nouwen
- Experiencing Father's Embrace – Jack Frost

Inner Healing & Emotional Wholeness
- Emotionally Healthy Spirituality – Peter Scazzero
- Healing the Soul of a Woman – Joyce Meyer
- The Bondage Breaker – Neil T. Anderson
- Victory Over the Darkness – Neil T. Anderson

Intimacy, Prayer & Presence

- Secrets of the Secret Place – Bob Sorge
- Hosting the Presence – Bill Johnson
- Draw the Circle – Mark Batterson
- Fervent – Priscilla Shirer

Spiritual Growth & Discipleship

- The Purpose Driven Life – Rick Warren
- The Spirit-Filled Life – Charles F. Stanley
- Celebration of Discipline – Richard Foster
- The Pursuit of God – A.W. Tozer

References and Acknowledgments

Scripture References

All Scripture quotations are taken from the **New King James Version®
(NKJV)** of the Bible, unless otherwise noted.

The following verses are referenced throughout this devotional:

Genesis 1:31; 3:15; 9:13–16
Exodus 34:6
Deuteronomy 7:9; 31:6
Psalm 30:5; 103:8; 136:1; 145:8–9
Proverbs 31
Isaiah 49:15–16; 54:10
Jeremiah 1:5; 31:3
Hosea 11:4
Matthew 22:37–39
John 3:16; 15:13
Romans 5:8; 8:38–39
1 Corinthians 13:8
Ephesians 2:4–5; 3:17–19
Philippians 1:9
1 John 4:9–10; 16; 19
Titus 2:7

Theological and Devotional Themes

The devotional content includes thematic references rooted in Christian prophetic and devotional tradition:

- **The Hannah Anointing** – Inspired by the story in *1 Samuel 1–2*, this phrase is commonly used in prophetic circles to describe intercession, perseverance, and birthing destiny through prayer.
- **The Secret Place** – Based on *Psalm 91:1*, this theme is explored in devotional literature that emphasizes intimate, personal communion with God.

Notable authors and works that reflect these themes include:

- Jeanne Guyon, *Experiencing the Depths of Jesus Christ*, Whitaker House
- Cindy Trimm, *Commanding Your Morning*, Charisma House
- Bill Johnson, *Hosting the Presence*, Destiny Image

Acknowledgments

I extend my heartfelt gratitude to:

- **Abba, My Heavenly Father**, the source and anchor of this work.

- **My earthly father, Hilton Cheevers**, whose steadfast example continues to inspire me.

- **Pastor Christopher Ibe**, a true father in the Lord, thank you for your leadership and covering.

- **Tony Brown (L.E.E. Apostolic Network)**, thank you for your powerful words in the foreword and your friendship.

- **Anita R. Minniefield**, for editing with excellence and grace.

To the family, friends, and destiny helpers who interceded, supported, and believed in this work—thank you.

May the love of the Father, revealed through every word, lead you into a deeper experience of His presence and peace.

About the Author

Dr. Lyn C. Inah is a seasoned leader, teacher, and intercessor with nearly 30 years of experience spanning both faith-based ministry and professional leadership. She earned a Doctor of Education in Adult, Community, and Higher Education Administration, as well as a Master of Divinity. Her life's work is devoted to equipping others for spiritual growth, effective leadership, and lasting transformation.

An ordained Itinerant Elder in the Lord's Church, Dr. Lyn is affirmed as a Five-Fold Ministry Gift to the Body of Christ. She has served faithfully in mid-size to large urban assemblies of Believers as Director of Pastoral Care, Welfare, and Community Outreach, and as Director of Christian Education. In these roles, she led initiatives that nurtured both the spiritual and practical well-being of individuals and communities. Her ministry is grounded in prayerful strategy, prophetic intercession, and a heart committed to healing, restoration, and renewal.

Dr. Lyn is the Founder and Chief Learning Officer of the Beacon Executive Leadership Institute, where she mentors and develops emerging, mid-level, and entry-level executive leaders. She blends biblical principles with leadership development strategies to guide others into their God-ordained purpose.

In the public sector, she served for more than 14 years as a Learning and Development Professional within the Executive Branch of the U.S. Federal Government. She is also a certified leadership coach, credentialed by the International Coaching Federation, the John Maxwell Team, and Gallup.

A native of Sylvester, Georgia, Dr. Lyn is married to Pastor Leo Fisher "Don" Inah. They are blessed with children, grandchildren, and a growing legacy of spiritual sons and daughters. This devotional reflects her heart to help others rest securely in the unfailing love of God the Father.